Will Muffins Find a Forever Family?

By Sha'Ronda Walton

Illustrated by Sari Prawita

Will Muffins Find A Forever Family?

Copyright © 2021 Sha'Ronda Walton

Contact the Author
sharonda.walton@yahoo.com

ISBN: 979-8-9851447-0-3

Printed in the United States of America

Hello, my name is Muffins, and this is my home.

I live in a shelter and I want a family of my own.

Here is where I sleep and stay.

The staff takes me out to potty and play.

I am waiting and wondering if today is the day.
Will they pick me, or will I stay?

What if I accidentally potty on the floor?

Will they throw me out of the front door?

Will they love me in every way, or will I have to find another place to stay?

I am dreaming of a home where I can run and play.
No matter what happens, they'll love me anyway.

People will be coming to the shelter today.

I am practicing my commands to sit and stay.

Someone is coming! I hear them say; we are looking for the cute little puppy we saw on your website yesterday.

She is a little tan dog with a curly tail and big brown eyes. What a surprise it is me they describe!

They take me out for a meet and greet.

I like this family; they look really neat.

There is a lady, a little girl and a dog just like me.

I hope and pray they like me.

They fill out the paper and pay the fee.

I hear the lady promise to take good care of me.

What a great day!
Today is the day. I finally found my forever family hooray!